For my jewels Noah, Milo, Zen and Lotus
For my mom Katharyn and Nefeterius
and, of course, for the ancestors —T.P.

I'd like to dedicate this to my mother, Stephanie Vann —J.O.

www.theenglishschoolhouse.com

Text copyright © 2018 by Tamara Pizzoli
Pictures copyright © 2018 by Jamilla Okubo
All rights reserved.

ISBN: 978-0-9976860-5-0

Jewels from Our Ancestors

A Book of African Proverbs
by Dr. Tamara Pizzoli

Illustrated by Jamilla Okubo

THE ENGLISH SCHOOL HOUSE

A fight
between
grasshoppers
is a joy
to the crow.

A united
family
eats from
the same
plate.

If you watch
your pot,
your food
will not burn.

A large chair does not make a King.

Good words
are food,
bad words
are poison.

One
who causes
others
misfortune
also
teaches them
wisdom.

Eat when
the food
is ready,
speak when
the time
is right.

Hold
a true friend
with both
hands.

The axe
forgets,
the tree
remembers.

Patience
can cook
a stone.

It's the
crooked
wood
that shows
the best
sculptor.

Do not
refuse a wing
to the person
who gave you
a full chicken.

Show me
your friend
and
I'll show you
your character.

Having
a good
discussion
is like
having
riches.

A
beautiful
thing
is

never

perfect.

He who
loves the vase
also loves
what is inside.